A box for Nan and Pop

Mum and Dan will go to Nan and Pop's.

Mum packs a box.
She has socks for Pop
and fig jam for Nan.

Dan picks up
the box.

At Nan and Pop's,
Dan and Mum
get a kiss.

10

Pop picks up the box.

The lid of the box pops up. It is Sid!

A box for Nan and Pop

Before reading

Say the sounds: c k ck j qu v w x y z zz ff ll ss

Practise blending the sounds: box pack packs socks jam picks kiss rock cat

High-frequency words: a Mum will up at get in it did not has is
Tricky words: for and go to she the no
Vocabulary check: fig – a sweet fruit that can be used to make jam

Story discussion: What is Pop doing? What might be in the box?

Teaching points: Check that children can read the graphemes c, ck, j, w, x, ll, ss. Pick one or two of these graphemes and ask children to find and read a word with each in the book. Check that they can make a sensible prediction about what might be in the box. Check that children can identify and read the tricky words: for, and, go, to, she, the, no.

After reading

Comprehension:
- Who visits Nan and Pop?
- What does Mum put in the box for Nan?
- Does Pop find it easy to pick up the box?
- What is the surprise at the end of the story?

Fluency: Speed-read the words again from the inside front cover.